Puerto Rico
The Isle of Enchantment

Marcia Amidon Lusted

PowerKiDS press™

New York

Published in 2011 by The Rosen Publishing Group, Inc.
29 East 21st Street, New York, NY 10010

First Edition

Editor: Maggie Murphy
Book Design: Greg Tucker
Photo Researcher: Jessica Gerweck

Photo Credits: Cover, pp. 9, 17, 22 (tree, frog, flower) Shutterstock.com; p. 5 A. Bello/Getty Images; p. 7 Buyenlarge/Getty Images; p. 11 © Rolf Nussbaumer/age fotostock; p. 13 Chase Jarvis/Getty Images; p. 15 altrendo nature/Getty Images; p. 19 Tom Bean/Getty Images; p. 22 (bird) © FLPA/age fotostock; p. 22 (seal) © Wikimedia Commons; p. 22 (Rita Moreno) Steve Granitz/WireImage/Getty Images; p. 22 (Roberto Clemente) MLB Photos via Getty Images; p. 22 (Joaquin Phoenix) Jeffrey Mayer/WireImage/Getty Images.

Library of Congress Cataloging-in-Publication Data

Lusted, Marcia Amidon.
  Puerto Rico : the Isle of Enchantment / Marcia Amidon Lusted. — 1st ed.
      p. cm. — (Our amazing states)
  Includes index.
  ISBN 978-1-4488-0668-3 (library binding) — ISBN 978-1-4488-0775-8 (pbk.) — ISBN 978-1-4488-0776-5 (6-pack)
  1. Puerto Rico—Juvenile literature. I. Title.
  F1958.3.L87 2011
  972.95—dc22
                                        2010005107

Manufactured in the United States of America

CPSIA Compliance Information: Batch #WS10PK: For Further Information contact Rosen Publishing, New York, New York at 1-800-237-9932

Contents

Welcome to the Isle of Enchantment

This place is not a state, but a **commonwealth**, of the United States. Both Spanish and English are spoken here. It is sometimes called *la isla del encanto*, or the isle of **enchantment**. Where are we? We are in Puerto Rico!

Puerto Rico, which means "rich port," in Spanish, is an **archipelago** in the Caribbean Sea. There is a larger main island and a number of smaller islands, including Vieques, Culebra, and Mona. They are located southeast of Florida and east of Cuba and Haiti. Puerto Rico is part of a group of islands called the Greater Antilles.

As a commonwealth of the United States, Puerto Rico has its own government. However, the United States has some control over that government.

Today many Puerto Ricans call the main island Borinquen, after the native Puerto Rican name for the island, Borikén.

Land of the Taino

Spanish **explorers**, led by Christopher Columbus, arrived in present-day Puerto Rico in 1493. They were looking for gold. The Spanish found Taino Indians living on the main island. The Tainos called it Borikén. Soon, the Spanish claimed the island for their country and forced the Tainos into slavery.

The island was an important port for the Spanish. It became a base for their navy. The Spanish renamed the island Puerto Rico. The Spanish also brought many African slaves there to look for gold after many Tainos died.

After the Spanish-American War, in 1898, the United States took control of Puerto Rico. Today it is a U.S. commonwealth, although some people would like it to become an official state.

This painting shows a battle between the U.S. Navy and Spanish forces off the coast of San Juan, Puerto Rico, in 1898. The battle was part of the Spanish-American War.

Rain Forests and Hurricanes

Puerto Rico is the smallest main island in the Caribbean Sea's Greater Antilles group, which includes Cuba, Haiti, and the Dominican Republic.

The Cordillera Central mountain range crosses the island from east to west. Rain forests cover its slopes. The karst region has **limestone** rock that has been worn away by rain, making sinkholes, cliffs, and caves. Sandy beaches ring the island.

Puerto Rico has a **tropical** climate. It is warm, sunny, and humid for most of the year. The island gets plenty of rain. Most of the rain comes during hurricane season, from May to October. Puerto Rico has been hit by many strong hurricanes. The word "hurricane" even comes from the name of the Taino storm god, Jurakán.

The limestone cliffs near Cabo Rojo, on the southwestern coast of Puerto Rico, are shown here. These cliffs rise about 200 feet (61 m) above the sea.

Under the Kapok Tree

Because of its tropical climate, Puerto Rico has many unusual plants and trees. The tall kapok tree is shaped like an umbrella. Breadfruit, mahogany, and coconut palm trees also grow on the island. The poinciana, a shrub with beautiful red blossoms, grows there as well.

Some of Puerto Rico's animals are rarely found anywhere else in the world. One of these animals is a tiny tree frog called the coquí. Another rare animal, the Puerto Rican parrot, is found only in hidden areas of the rain forest. However, lizards and bats can be found all over the island. In the nineteenth century, mongooses were brought to the island to control rats on sugar **plantations**. They can still be found there today.

Here you can see a kind of hummingbird called an Antillean mango feeding on a banana blossom in Luquillo, Puerto Rico.

What Do People Do in Puerto Rico?

Before 1950, Puerto Rico's biggest business was producing sugar from a plant called sugar cane. It was grown on huge plantations. Today farmers grow coffee, pineapples, mangoes, and citrus fruit. However, most people on the island work in the service **industry**. The companies they work for provide a service for others, such as financial services and communications.

Some companies in Puerto Rico make clothing, chemicals, and electronics. The most important product made in Puerto Rico is medical drugs. Many companies that make medicine have factories there. The island also makes money from visitors. Millions of people visit every year and need places to eat and stay and things to do for fun.

One of Puerto Rico's biggest crops is coffee. Here, bags of coffee beans sit in a warehouse, ready to be sold in Puerto Rico and many other places.

A Bay Full of Stars

Off the coast of Puerto Rico is a small island called Vieques. The Spanish built their last fort in the New World, the Fort Count Mirasol, there. Later, the U.S. Navy bought most of Vieques and tested weapons there. Today there is a wildlife **refuge** there. Wild horses run free on the island.

Vieques has beautiful beaches with white sand and blue water. These beaches are still known by the names the U.S. Navy gave to them, such as the Blue Beach, the Red Beach, and the Green Beach. However, Vieques is most famous for its **bioluminescent** bay. There, tiny **organisms** give off a bright blue glow when they move around. At night, this glow makes the bay look like it is filled with stars.

Here you can see many yellow wrasses, which are a kind of fish, swimming around Angel Reef, off the coast of Vieques.

Seeing San Juan

Puerto Rico's capital is San Juan. The oldest part of the city, Old San Juan, was settled by the Spanish in 1509 and surrounded by tall stone walls. The Spanish once guarded the city from two forts, El Morro and Castillo de San Cristobál, which can still be visited today. San Juan is also a busy modern port and a business center. Many factories for **processing** petroleum and sugar are found there.

There are many interesting things to see in San Juan. You can visit the **plazas** of the old city and see many statues. You can also walk through the Parque de las Palomas, located on top of the city wall. The Museo del Indio features displays on Puerto Rico's native peoples.

The chapel of the San Juan Cemetery, shown here, was built in the late nineteenth century. In the background, you can see one of San Juan's famous forts, El Morro.

A Rain Forest Park

Puerto Rico is home to the only tropical rain forest in the U.S. National Forest system, El Yunque National Forest. It was once a special place for the Taino Indians. You can still see their ancient drawings, called petroglyphs, cut into river rocks.

The forest's Luquillo Mountains can get as much as 200 inches (508 cm) of rain every year. Thousands of rare tropical plants can be found there, as well as animals like the coquí and the Antillean ghost-faced bat. La Coca Falls flows down 85 feet (26 m) over large rocks covered in moss. Visitors can walk through the forest on an **elevated** walkway. There, they can see the forest from treetop level.

Here you can see bromeliads, a kind of rootless plant, growing in Puerto Rico's El Yunque National Forest.

Come to Puerto Rico!

Whether you like swimming in clear blue water or learning about Spanish explorers, Puerto Rico has something for you. You can see colorful costumes and masks at the St. James Festival in Loíza. You can also visit the Arecibo Observatory and see the largest radio **telescope** in the world. There, scientists have listened for signs of life on faraway planets.

If you love nature, you can hike through the rain forests and mountains. Perhaps you will even see a rare bird or a tiny tree frog there. You can also go kayaking in the glow of the bioluminescent bay. No matter what you like to do, Puerto Rico is a great place to visit or live!

Glossary

archipelago (ar-kih-PEH-luh-goh) A group of islands.

bioluminescent (by-oh-loo-muh-NEH-sent) Glowing with light made by a
living organism.

commonwealth (KAH-mun-welth) A nation or state founded on what is right for the
common good.

elevated (EH-leh-vayt-ed) Lifted above something.

enchantment (en-CHANT-ment) The condition of being very enjoyable or likeable.

explorers (ek-SPLOR-erz) People who travel and look for new land.

industry (IN-dus-tree) A business in which many people work and make money
producing a product.

limestone (LYM-stohn) A kind of rock made of the bodies of small ocean animals.

organisms (OR-guh-nih-zumz) Living beings made of dependent parts.

plantations (plan-TAY-shunz) Very large farms where crops are grown.

plazas (PLA-zuz) Public squares.

processing (PRAH-ses-ing) Treating or changing something using special steps.

refuge (REH-fyooj) A place where something is kept safe.

telescope (TEH-leh-skohp) An instrument used to study faraway objects.

tropical (TRAH-puh-kul) Having to do with the warm parts of Earth that are near
the equator.

Puerto Rico Symbols

Tree
Kapok Tree

Animal
Coquí

Commonwealth
Flag

Bird
Reinita Mora

Flower
Flor de Maga

Commonwealth
Seal

Famous People from Puerto Rico

Rita Moreno
(1931–)
Born in Humacao, PR
Actress/Singer

Roberto Clemente
(1934–1972)
Born in San Juan, PR
Baseball Player

Joaquin Phoenix
(1974–)
Born in San Juan, PR
Actor

Puerto Rico Map

Legend

⭕ Major City

⭐ Capital

〜 River

Atlantic Ocean

San Juan

Arecibo

Bayamón

Culebra

Cerro de Punta

Río de la Plata

Caguas

Grande de Loíza

Vieques

Cordillera Central

Mona

Ponce

Caribbean Sea

Puerto Rico Facts

Population: About 442,447

Area: 122 square miles (316 sq km)

Motto: "John Is His Name"

Song: "La Borinqueña," words by Manuel Fernández Juncos
and music by Luis Miranda

Index

C
climate, 8, 10
commonwealth, 4, 6
control, 4, 6, 10
Cuba, 4, 8
Culebra, 4

E
English, 4
explorers, 6, 20

F
factories, 12, 16
Florida, 4

G
government, 4
Greater Antilles, 4, 8

H
Haiti, 4, 8

I
island(s), 4, 6, 8, 10,
    12, 14

K
karst region, 8

L
limestone, 8

M
Mona, 4

O
organisms, 14

P
plantations, 10, 12
plazas, 16

S
Spanish, 4, 6, 14, 16,
    20

T
telescope, 20

V
Vieques, 4, 14
visitors, 12, 18

W
war, 6
wildlife refuge, 14

Web Sites

Due to the changing nature of Internet links, PowerKids Press has developed an online list of Web sites related to the subject of this book. This site is updated regularly. Please use this link to access the list:

www.powerkidslinks.com/amst/pr/

24